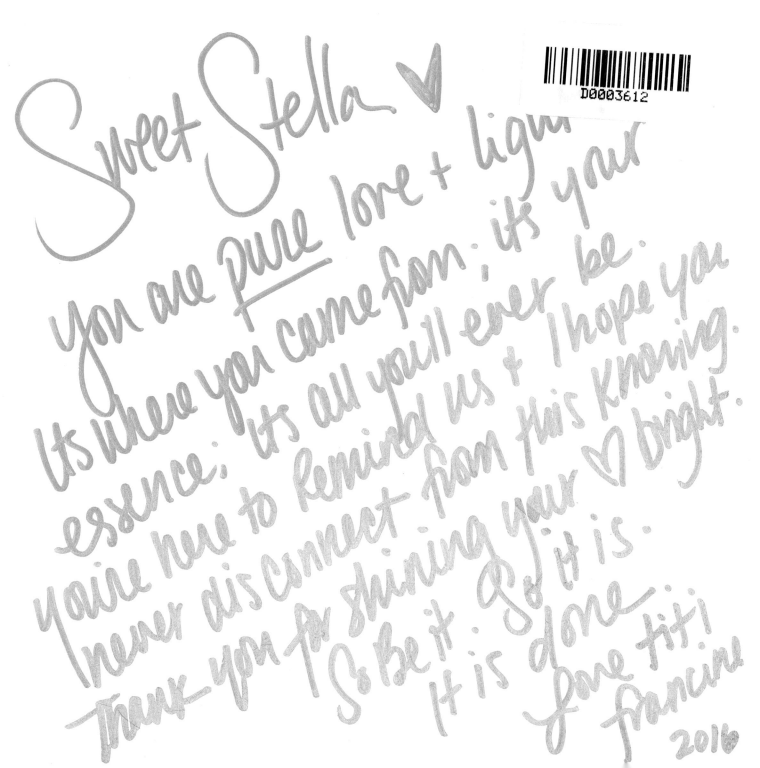

Sweet Stella ♡

You are pure love + light.
Its where you came from; its your
essence. Its all you'll ever be.
You're here to remind us + I hope you
never disconnect from this knowing.
Thank you for shining your ♡ bright.

So be it. So it is.
It is done. Love tit!
francine
2016

Love, Peace & Light

This book is dedicated to all the children in the world.
May you all live a life with love, peace and light.

With a special dedication to my daughters Katya & Daria
and much gratitude to Dr. Joseph Michael Levry, founder of Naam Yoga.

Text by Joseph Michael Levry
Creative Direction by Primavera Salvá
Illustrations by Isabelle Duverger

PROLOGUE

Nothing is more precious than Love. Working with Love is an action that is in total alignment with the Universe. Without Love, there will be no cosmos. The entire world is kept together by the energy of Love.

We come from Love, and we are nothing other than the manifestation of love. Love is our innate state. Love is our birthright.

By working with this meditation, we counteract some of the negative effects that can be around us and it allows us to set in motion positive effects by working with Love, Peace and Light.

I composed this simple, beautiful, and powerful meditation, so that anyone may use it to heal and elevate all beings in the world. Let all of us share our Love, Peace, and Light out unto the Earth, to the four corners of the planet, in order to raise its vibration and let the true light shine through.

Dr. Joseph Michael Levry

Hi!

My name is Shakti and this beautiful blue bird is my friend Vida.
Together we want to show a fun meditation!
This is a fun game to create Love, Peace and Light in you,
around you and in the entire Universe!

All you have to do is repeat the magic words I share with you
on each page and move your arms the way I am showing you
in the next pages. Vida will also help you to point what to do.

Have fun!

Shakti

love before me

love behind me

love at my left

love at my right

love below me

love in me

love in my surroundings

love to the Universe

peace before me

peace behind me

peace at my left

peace at my right

peace above me

peace below me

peace in me

peace in my surroundings

peace to all

peace to the Universe

light before me

light behind me

light at my left

light at my right

light above me

light below me

light in me

light in my surroundings

light to all

light to the Universe

Note to parents:
Love, Peace & Light is a meditation from Naam Yoga.
This book can be read to children as a bedtime story
or as a game following the arm movements.
Learn more about Love, Peace & Light movement at
www.lovepeacelighttoall.com

CPSIA information can be obtained
at www.ICGtesting.com
Printed in the USA
BVOW07*1935150716
455736BV00002B/4/P